INSPIRING GENERATIONS EXPRESSIONS TO A SOCIAL GENERATION

By N. Malaki Crayton

Inspire others and you yourself ...
...will be inspired

Published by

Midnight Express Books
POBox 69
Berryville, AR 72616

INSPIRING GENERATIONS EXPRESSIONS TO A SOCIAL GENERATION

By N. Malaki Crayton

INSPIRING GENERATIONS EXPRESSIONS TO A SOCIAL GENERATION

Published by

Midnight Express Books
POBox 69
Berryville, AR 72616

INSPIRING GENERATIONS EXPRESSIONS TO A SOCIAL GENERATION

ACKNOWLEDGEMENTS

All glory, honor, and respect belong to the Divine Creator of life. It is by this gift that we are appreciative of one another and our individuality within the collective.

Eternally grateful to, and for, my mother Denise Taylor; she is the one that has given me the sincere appreciation for life, women, and their role in this world.

To my brothers whom have guided me and corrected my errors, you are loved and honored:

David "Diesel" Jennings

Joseph "Bear" Starks

Dujuan "D-mac" Dixon

Ronald "Pinky/Yoab" Blackwell

Charles "Chuck" Murray

LaFarique "LA" Aubry

Christopher Coleman

Corey Drummond

Corey "Inspirational" West

Antonio Johnson

N. Malaki Crayton

Willie "Bo" Burgain

Rodney "Zelle" Cooks

Keion "Wise" Davis

Christopher Shakur Brown

Thank you for all of your continuous effort in our struggle against the chaotic conditioned mind that is laced in our world.

INTRODUCTION

There was a time when all of humanity worked in unison, when all were aligned with one language and one thought. Genesis, chapter 11, whether allegorical or historical, explains the uniqueness within this unity. If God knows that unity can achieve great feats, why is it so difficult for us to perceive this idea?

We are living in a new time as old ideas of racism, bigotry, and class-systems are dying away. People, especially the younger generations, are crossing all barriers and appreciating solidarity. More and more children are being born of mixed heritage, with no singular identity. So what does this make them? Outcasts, undesirables, hybrids? Certainly Not! They are reflections of a harmonious understanding within the human essence made physical.

Our one true duty that our Creator bestowed upon us was to live. Whether you follow one of the prominent religious sects or the smaller factions, the single apex in all of them is parallel. The Divine Spirit of God promotes life in all of humanity.

Humans are not sedentary beings. We are continuously in motion. Always striving for action or any time fulfilling itinerary, continuous in our societal activities, we invent the imaginative thought into reality. As humans, our imaginations illuminate our hopes, our desires, and expand our dreams. When we use our imaginations to create, our happiness is revealed.

Inspiration is about solidifying our purpose in unity. It is an action that truly means that we are doing good things to achieve a positive goal. We must be men and women that are living for the amelioration of the world. This does not impede our happiness, but manifest it tangibly for us. As more people are realizing that their happiness (Contentment, meaning that their desires are limited only in their appeasement) is either deterred or blossomed from within, has allowed a robust of inspiration to happen in the world.

Humans are interdependent. In China, America, or Latin America we do need the assistance of each other. Isolation does not work for any one person or nation. Humans are innately sociable and cannot truly be happy without interaction. This is part of our natural consciousness.

As a humanistic society, one of many shades and ideas, the common fabric, purpose that is in us will never change nor be impeded because we are all bound to it:

LIFE

Author's Note

There are nine numbers in our system (plus 0) and numbers always have a value other than what is seen. I've extracted some ideas that lie behind numbers 1-10. What are the correlations that you see in the world?

Contents

N. Malaki Crayton

PART I CONNECTIONS

N. Malaki Crayton

ONE

FIRST

ORIGIN

SOURCE

BEGINNING

N. Malaki Crayton

CHAPTER 1   GENESIS THEORY

The book of Genesis is seen as the origin or source of everything. It is incontestably without flaw according to the church. Although the scriptures have been translated numerous times by multiple people, it is seen as flawless. And while I do not contest the Infinites flawlessness, I do know that men make mistakes and attempt to fill in what is not understood.

Genesis seems to be ubiquitous at times but there is some specificity contained therein. While people have for the major part of our history argued over what is and what is not, the one consistent strain is evident that we are interwoven in our survival. Whatever the Divine intent upon our creation, it is certain that we are dependent upon one another and that our real experience, which God is recognized, is in our interactive treatment towards one another.

No matter who the so-called authoritarian is on any of these subjects, no one knows with certainty what happened. We speculate as to what happened in the beginning of creation so that our purpose will appear somewhat clearer. Our arrogance permits us to believe that everything in the universe surrounds us or must submit to us. Humans have a special type of arrogance that allows us to commit terror in the name of our faith. It allows us to believe that what we choose to do no matter how horribly extreme, is okay because the Divine favors us over everyone else. We all desire answers as to why things happen and we would all like to believe in a Creator that thinks particular about us personally.

This protection shields is from the harsh faces of our society. Believing in a God that will defend us even while we remain defiant is as satisfying as it is farcical.

There are some things that we are certain about: We die, we have a choice, and something greater than us created us (and imprinted a piece if itself onto us). This entire process within the scriptures is debatable because of its ambiguity and man's decisive maneuvers to manipulate. Many people have died and killed in the debate of the "WORD OF GOD". Everyone believes that they are doing the "WILL OF GOD", yet people always tell us that no one knows what God's will is. Funny though, Paul tells us in Ephesians 5:17, "Wherefore be ye not unwise, but understanding what the will of the Lord is." How can we understand something if we have no idea what it is? Maybe Its Will is imprinted upon us. If we are designed in the Creators', "image and Likeness", then how do we know that God's purpose is not built within us? Every designer puts his trademark/signature on the design, just as nothing is built that does not serve the motive of its Creator, whether it wants to or not. There are always safety protocols that designers make on their products, and death may be seen as a safety mechanism attached to us. Could you imagine how less we would appreciate life if it were limitless on this plain? How much more dangerous that our world could be if destructive people, with malicious ideas, did not die out?

The second chapter of Genesis begins with the completion of Creation. Look at the words within the first verse. Focus in on the words "Host of them". What exactly does this mean and who is the host? I've seen people to interpret this to mean stars, aliens, or angels. But none of these made sense to me. The Hebrew word that is transliterated into host is 'zaba, which literally translates as

4

"throng or mass of people". You can look this up in any concordance or dictionary and it will be the same. There is not a separate or dual meaning for this word. it means a mass of people, a lot of people. So, how is this hidden from the translators and the scholars that have been over these doctrines for years? That's the issue. It hasn't been hidden. It just does not complement the stories that have been taught but it does explain why Cain was so afraid when he slew his brother and why he was able to marry (Genesis 4:17). There had to have been other people there at that time.

Another complicated verse is that of chapter 2. In it, it says that God had completed his "work" that he had been doing. The word here is not the standard word for work (which is Avodah). Here, the word used is Malakto, which is more like "His message" or "his ministers". This is not corresponding to the type of work as if to say, making a universe.

Now down in chapter 4, we are told that this is the history of the Heavens and the Earth. The word used for story is Toledot, which is more accurately translated as, generations. These are the generations of the heavens and the earth. Remember, man did not become a living being until the Divine breathed life into him. Man is part earth and part Divine energy.

Chapter 2

1. Thus the heavens and the earth were finished, and all the host of them.

2. And on the seventh day, God ended his work which he had made; and he rested on the seventh day from all his work which he had made.

3. And God blessed the seventh day, and sanctified it: because that in it he had rested from all his work which God created and made.

4. These are the generations of the heavens and the earth when they were created, in the day that the Lord God made the earth and the heavens.

If the word for people is used here, then maybe there were more than two people. This would make sense from a practical position.

Maybe this is not the creation of the universe solely but a new system of organization. A new beginning in our history that was better fit to lead us into a more intimate stage with our Creator. The repoire between God and Adam is almost familiar with our idea of a proper father teaching and nurturing a child. This relationship pivots us into a responsibility role with everything in the universe. When we don't appreciate the rest of creation as having the spirit of the Divine within it, we are disrespectful to the One that created us all. I respect my father but I don't respect the house that he built. Evident in the way that we treat one another, how do you say, "I love my dad but I hate my brothers and sisters?" Really? But they are your father, just as you are (and Mother as well). Not appreciating life because its duty is not as visible as yours is arrogant and selfish.

Another totally unacceptable breakage in the law that we allow comes in the form of misogyny. Woman's role in the perfection of the universe is probably the most disrespectful and facetiously pounced upon in our time. It is pure suicide to inhibit our partners from performing their duties, especially when it is for the betterment of the human family. The balance must be respected.

Everyone must be allowed to perform their duties or we will all fail.

Here we have the inception of woman. The importance of woman is clearly expressed in this chapter.

GENESIS 2:21-24

> "And the Lord God caused a deep sleep to fall upon Adam, and he slept: and He took one of his ribs, and closed up the flesh thereof;
>
> And the rib, which the Lord God had taken from man, made Him a woman, and brought her unto man.
>
> And Adam said," This is now bone of my bones, and flesh of my flesh; she shall be called woman, because she was taken out of man.
>
> Therefore shall a man leave his father and his mother, and shall cleave unto his wife: and they shall be one flesh."

It is clear that man was not supposed to live by himself and that woman was made to aid him. To help him do what was not exactly defined (except have dominion over the earth; caretaker), but when we look further down upon woman's creation, we can extrapolate her position. The scriptures state that she was created from the rib. Why the rib? This doesn't appear to be a particularly romantic form of creation, as say, the heart. But further study upon the rib is actually astonishing. When you take a look at the ribs, they are critical to a person's existence. The physical rib actually has a great function. What does it do? Protect! It protects the heart and the lungs. Vital organs to life. The ribs are the defense barrier from the outside forces that may threaten the function of the body. They deflect the impact of the strike's and blows that attempt to harm man. Now, if women are a product of this, then that means that she protects the inner most vulnerable part of man, his heart/mind. She is the one that gives him stability. She protects him from all outside influences and his own inner hubris (his own exaggerated selfishness). She is in fact his balance. She protects him from the things that he does not realize about himself. Woman, in fact, is very strong because she harbors a sufficient amount of patience. She completes him because she protects him. Man and woman complement each other as a perfectly combined force. Women's position have been stripped from them. Their duties as protectors have been taken from them and they have been demoralized to the position of subservient. This is not their defining duty, although we attempt to bind them to such.

Why would the Divine create a "tree" of knowledge of good and evil? Simply to test Adam? Knowing everything, why would God banish them for something he knew they would do?

We all have some understanding about the story of Adam and Eve. They fell because they ate from the tree of good and evil. Eve deceived her husband. Simple as that, right? Not exactly. Did Eve really attempt to deceive her husband? No. Genesis, chapter 3, verse tells us that she believed that the tree was good, and that it would make him smart. Now, if I'm trying to trick someone, I'm surely not going to give them something that will make them smarter. That is not sensible. Remember, she was created to be a helper, she is a part of him, so what does she gain by hurting him, which in turn hurts her. It does not imply that she walked away from Adam when the serpent gave her the fruit nor does it say that she was alone. She gave it to the man with her. She thought that she was helping him, as was her duty.

Of course this was clear disobedience but whose disobedience?

Adam was told explicitly not to touch the fruit of that tree yet he did so anyway. The punishment for Eve is expressed in her child-bearing description. The scriptures say that her desire will be for her husband always. This is not an oppressive type relationship. Adam's punishment is described in verse 17 when he is admonish-ed about his disobedience. The ground has been cursed on his be-half and it must be toiled for repayment. Ultimately, his punish-ment is settled in his eventual return to the ground.

Now, I don't know about you but if someone had lied to me (that was suppose to help me), and caused me to be punished by death, I would not be so forgiving. Adam named her Chavah (Eve), the Mother of Life. That is very powerful. I don't think that I would be calling someone by the name of life had they brought death upon me.

Let us look at their eviction. It is normally accepted that they were sent out of the garden because of disobedience, but that is not accurate.

Genesis 22-23

> "And the Lord God said, Behold, the man is *become* as one of us, to know good and evil: and now, lest he put forth his hand, and take

also of the tree of life, and eat, and live
forever:

Therefore the Lord God sent him forth from the Garden of Eden to
till the ground from whence he was taken. He became a threat
when he obtained the knowledge of good and evil. People say that
Adam was given a death sentence when he ate of the fruit but if
God was worried about him eating from the tree of life (which
would give him eternal life) then he could not have had eternal life
in the beginning. So that means that death was always there. He
was driven away essentially for what he may become."

The legacy of Cain and Abel comes into question as well. We
know the story. Jealousy and murder. But it was only Cain's in-
eptness that allowed God's favor to pass over him. If he'd applied
himself, then jealousy would not have had room to maneuver in his
mind. God told him in verse 7, that sin waits for an opening, and to
you it comes, but YOU CAN MASTER IT. This is the CREATOR
OF ALL THINGS telling him that he can control his ability to
receive sin. I'm not implying that people will not do things that are
contradictive or implement things that hurt them, but I do believe
that this power to combat these decisions lies within the spirit of
the individual.

When Adam took of the tree of knowledge of good and evil, he
was able to perceive, not just see. His mind was opened and he was
aware of all things. This was dangerous for him and the environment around him. We build upon bad ideas as well as good. Once
multiple ideas were implemented into his mind, this opened the
option for bad choices. Too many conflicting questions and ideas
floating around permitted arrogance and doubt to enter. This allowed him more of an option to break the established standards set

by God. So, does real freedom come with allowing people to do whatever they want, or just whatever they want within a set of parameters? We all believe that we do not need to be told what to do or "watched over", yet even some of the most blameless people have committed less than grandiose acts. Human predictability is so common that we have become unaware and shocked by it. The Bible, the Qu'ran, the Tao, the Sanskrit, are all repetitive. They repeat themselves with a boldness that echoes throughout our cultures.

All of these examples are simply standards for us to understand the laws that were given by an infinite being. The rules set forth are not magical. They have a specific purpose and are expected to be respected. All people suffer when we ignore the universal principles. Simply ask yourself, are you seeing life with the sincere spirit that is in everything or are you looking through someone else's perspective for their purpose? Remember, you and no one else will answer for your mistakes and your salvation. You are responsible for your duty in this world.

N. Malaki Crayton

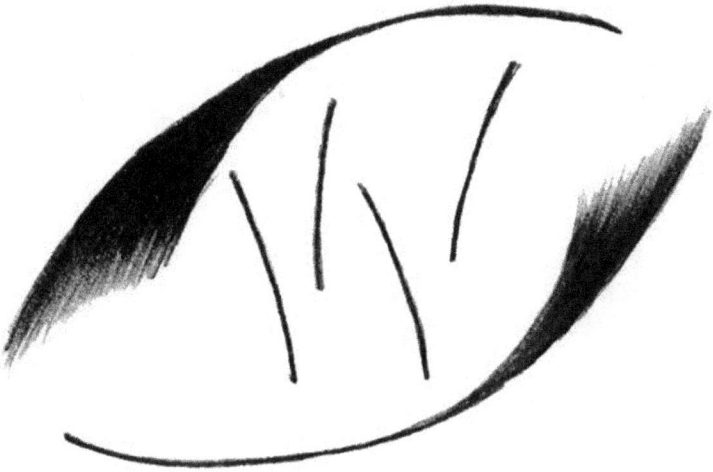

TWO

PARTNERS

A PAIR

DUALITY

UNITY

N. Malaki Crayton

CHAPTER 2 INSTRUCTIONS

Universal laws have no expiration date upon them. They do not fade because of inactivity and there is no repeal when it comes to the infinite design. They do not become void because we do not believe in their existence. They are here to preserve you. They are made because human behavior is predictable. You believe that you are not predictable? That you are spontaneous and can never be lured into the cycle of behavior? Really? We are all designed with an innate system of fallacy. one that allows us to make mistakes in our perfection (because you are designed perfect, complete, whole).

There are addictions that lie within all of us whether they are of touch, taste, feeling, money, or arrogance, there is something that you are subject to in your life. It may not be that noticeable to you, but there are people in your life that can see it.

Humans adapt. We can adapt to the most terrible conditions or become acclimated into a new society without confliction. This ability has allowed us to persevere and create societies that con-tinuously evolve despite our fallacies. We have so many laws and rules that they can seem overwhelming but you must consider that rules are only designed for something in which there is a demand for. As far as I know, there is a "no littering" policy in every state, why? Well, because people have a lazy tendency to throw garbage on the ground, even when there is a trash can two feet away. Garbage on the street not only devalues the neighborhood financially, but psychologically (people are depressed in filth), and socially (people are seen as undesirables). Laws are there to preserve and protect (no matter how we may perceive them).

But what does this really mean to you. I mean, it sounds good as an idea but how do you really practice it? How does this protect you? Quotes and sayings always sound fantastic when you first read them. Your neurons light up and you become excited. Then comes the action part and all of those twinkly lights and feelings disappear. Those "great sayings" appear to be ridiculing you and they become burdensome. The thing is, instructions are not there just to make your life easy. They are tests that have been performed and are put in place so that you don't screw up and kill yourself (or someone else). They are to prevent you from hurting yourself unnecessarily. Instructions allow you to see into the past to become more efficient in the future. When they are explained, you can see what befell your predecessor, and if they are concise, then you can see what will happen if you oppose them. They act as buffers, so to speak.

The human desire to live is concurrent with God's desire for is to live through Its instructions. The Creator allows us the passion to live, so to aid in that is not wrong. The Divine points us to the direction of life and if medicines, surgeries, or meditation assists in that, who are we to contest that. We tend to forget that the Creator is the one that gave us this intelligence. There are natural elements in the earth that heal us. Should these be shunned as prohibited devices? Or should they be recognized as part of the harmonic cycle that adheres to the balance. We understand that everything dies eventually but everything needn't die right now. Our designer has given us the intelligence to achieve great feats. To squander this gift is not only disrespectful, but threatening to our survival. We are not smarter than the Infinite Source. Whatever your choices in life, there is still a requirement for you to follow the

Divine rules that are set. In all religious beliefs, all perspectives, there are instructions that none of us can avoid. The book of Job says that you can "Speak to the earth and it will teach you" (12:8). The Hebrew is more accurate in saying to "meditate (become one with) the earth and it will instruct you". If we are physically from the earth, every mineral, every element, then that means that our bodies react just as the earth does. We are a physical entity with an innate spirit, so why would you not believe that the earth is the same.

We must stop thinking with an oppressed mind. Our perspectives of freedom and slavery are becoming blurred and so we complain and whine when we feel as though the world is not designed to our advantage. We are not stolid beings and should not act as if we do not require instructions. When people think of instructions, they think of restrictions. They think of more rules to oppress their already depressed lives. Even when some people see an instructions label on the side of a box, they are deterred from reading it because it seems more like a chore than an advisor.

We are a part of life. We are life. There are not numerous paths to life. There is life and there is death. That is absolute. That is the balance. We are born, experience, breed, work, express, appreciate, accept, and then expire back into the existence that is the Divine. What we are doing while here is to live within the balance without offsetting ourselves. There is a balance. One that you feel every day. One that lets you know when you have come into the threshold of pain, affliction, or consciousness. These are not abnormalities that just happen. It is designed, systematically, strategically, to be an alert system for you. Do not ignore your connection to and with everything around and in you.

Societies have always worked within a system. Whether it was established for security, order, or economic benefit, there has always been a need for checks and balancing in a system. You are a single example of this system. You have things that check and balance you out. Those things that allow you to live. When you get hurt, your system automatically repairs this area. If an infection occurs, your immune system attacks the invader. When there is danger, your neurons are set off and a feeling of fear comes upon you. You are a perfectly working system, no matter how you may think that you are flawed. You are perfection, completion, but you must also respect the unseen order that is established in the world.

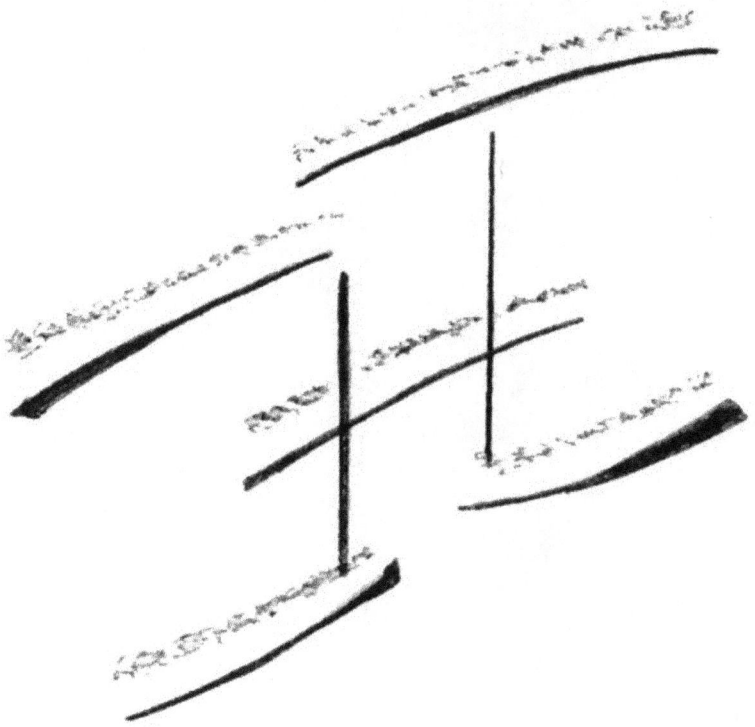

THREE

FAMILY

TRINITY

N. Malaki Crayton

CHAPTER 3   HUMANITY

JUST BECAUSE SOMEONE HATES ME FOR MY HUE DOES
NOT MEAN THAT I AM TO HATE THEM FOR THEIRS.

Religion is an important aspect in many of our lives. We are
admonished of terrific stories that inspire triumphant victories
through fearless people of an unchangeable and unquestionable
God. We are taught that "blind faith" is the ultimate form of
worship and to ask questions would be direct defiance to our deity,
only to be punished with an unfathomable torment.

We have inherited these stories that have been passed down for
thousands of years. Forever molded into the fabric of our minds.
We are to fear a Creator whom we cannot seek yet hold a personal
relationship with one that we can never know. I am a believer in
the Divine, the Infinite, the Intelligent. I am not a believer in
Myths, Mysteries, or stereotypes. I believe that the Divine Creator
has installed within humans the ability to think and extract information out of the environment, and more importantly,
ourselves. Although we may not be able to rationalize the Infinite
Intelligence that is our designer, it did give us the ability to
conceptualize each other and our duties to one another. The Divine
is shown through us when we connect, locking in our spirit. The
Divine did not whisper to us in secret (Isaiah 45:19). It was bold,
defining, and clear. The Divine is the balance within the Universe
and in all of us. According to the Book of Isaiah (45:7), the Creator
is the designer of all things, those that we like and those that we do
not. God did not stumble upon evil within Lucifer as if It did not
know that it existed. How could the Divine be Infinite and

Omniscient if it did not perceive evil? That is not in accordance with what is revealed.

We must stop pretending to act as if people do not control what they do (granted there are some medical symptoms that inhibit sound decisions). We refuse to look at what we are all capable of. Look at our cinema for example. We see some of the most mild, humble people play some of the most outrageous, spiteful villains (and they do an outstanding job). Why do you think that this is? Acting school? Good skills? Or is it that we all possess the innate ability to be the best or the worst. All humans are capable of being wicked. People would like to restrict horrible acts (such as slavery, genocide, murder) to one set of people, but as history shows us, this is not true. All countries have their shame. All tribes have their shadows in which they are not proud of. But does this make us more different or more similar? Does the ability to be civil only lie in the west or a Democratic society?

Our humanity does not reside simply in our ability to act "civil" with each other. Our humanity is revealed when we recognize that connecting spark, that linking spirit that is breathed in and out of all of us. We all share the Divine Breath of the Creator and that is who and what we must see when dealing with each other. There is more than just the evident physical connection that we should see, but the unseen correlation that intertwines us all.

America is supposed to represent the world unifying in common fundamentals and ideals. For all of our deficiencies, our disagreements, and our dislikes, we still live in tolerance of one another. But tolerance can only hold for a specified amount of time. We must evolve from tolerance to recognition (gratitude or acknowledgement of one another). We must recognize that none of us hold dominance over this planet. None of us will rule forever on this land. None of our kingdoms, dynasties, or policies will outlive the earth. We are interdependent upon one another as we are dependent upon the planet. This is our home, not our conquest.

We are all linked to the same energy that flows throughout all living things. You are connected to the trees that you walk pass every day. The sun that is so far away yet is so necessary for life to begin (and endure). The ocean that is so powerful that it is needed for its balance and cleansing abilities. The air, which we all share, is not so different in any part of the world (except when we pollute it). What does it take for humans to feel that impulsive surge of life? Many times, a tragedy, but more effectively, a realization or alertness to the fragility of life.

All cultures on this planet have contributed something to this world. Some may see it as trivial but it cannot be torn from the fabric of this world. Everyday our presence is imprinted upon the reality of historical existence. We are here and we have our positions to uphold. In unity, we accomplish everything, separated, we default on our loan which is the Universal Spirit. We are collectively involved with one another, whether we want to be or not.

We cannot isolate ourselves from each other. That is not how we will survive. That is not how we are designed. We are built as social, interactive beings that require contact to live.

GENESIS 11:1, 6

> 1. "Now the whole earth was of one language and one speech,"

> 6. "And the Lord said," Surely the people

are one and they all have one tongue, and this is what they begin to do; Now nothing that they propose to do will be withheld from them."

If this scripture is proposed to be true then what is realized is that as a unit, we are perfect. Language is the greatest barrier that impedes our interaction. As a living unit, we are collectively strong. When some fall short, others spiral into action making up the difference. When there is a crisis, our innate human reaction propels us to do what is necessary.

Humans have an amazing ability to adapt and survive. This gift has allowed us (from the Creator) to persevere this long. Who do we really think that we are to do anything without the assistance of God or each other? Arrogance gives permission for error to come into our presence. Human arrogance is dangerous and disastrous because it assumes, exaggerates, and separates. The things that divide us are so ridiculous at times that it is not even humorous.

The Creator gave us all a gift that is taken for granted because we show not enough appreciation for the things that were created, including and especially, other people.

FOUR

CORNERS

SUBMISSION

A BEAST

CHAPTER 4   RESPONSIBILITY

The word responsibility has taken on a bad connotation in this new age. Too many of us equate responsibility with guilt. People are afraid to accept responsibility for fear of being penalized, ridiculed, or they simply fear failing. We flee from it so that we can find security in "plausible deniability". What a farce! In this western world of ideological principles, we place so much emphasis on the Bible but we continue to ignore many of its instructions.

PROVERBS 3:27-30

> "Withhold not good from them to whom it is due, when it is in the power of thine hand to do it.
>
> Say not unto thy neighbor, go, and come again, and tomorrow I will give; when thou hast it by thee.
>
> Devise not evil against thy neighbor, seeing he dwelleth securely by thee.
>
> Strive not with a man without cause, if he have done thee no harm."

These are not vague, ubiquitous words that are not clear. If you have the ability to do good, do it! If you have the ability to help someone now, don't wait until tomorrow. Do not be angry or spiteful with people that have done nothing to you. Oh you don't do this? Just about everyone has done it. Whether you have despised someone for being more attractive than you, or maybe you have just encouraged a rumor that was already in play. We are a gossip capital, which means that everyone is watching everyone, looking for something to report. We must stop hurting each other for fun and publicity. We say that we are the most civilized nation on the planet. Well, civilized people are responsible, dependable.

Responsibility is a compassionate characteristic. It is a Divine attribute that says, "I care and accept the choice". This trait requires courage when it is attacked, strength when it is pressured, and support when it absorbs a mistake (conflict). Stop allowing your fears to make you submit. People are afraid when they have never experienced something or when there is uncertainty. But there is a certainty in your ability to perform a task (duty). Have the courage to embrace your skills and your ability to perform tasks without deceit and fraud. When you exhibit your genuineness and sincerity, people will respond more favorably if you are not found corrupt. There is no trick or scheme to accepting your role (even in failure) and people will see the Truth revealed through you. Lies are only allowed so many outfits to change before they are exposed. That is just a natural law. No one is superior to the intellect of the Infinite, thus all corruption becomes revealed because there are limits to what people will tolerate.

We blame everyone and everything else for the crap that happens in our lives. The blunderous errors that we knew that we should not have engaged in yet we allowed our lusts to carry us onward into the trap. Our responsibility must be accepted and enacted. It is very easy (and draining) to complain. Continuously speaking about what someone else needs to do in order to correct their deficiencies, yet we seem unable, or inept, to correct our own. Are we simply hypocrites that can allot information but unable to apply it in real life? Hardly. We choose to be hypocrites because it is the the norm. Because it is what we are used to in a world where no one can be trusted. People will always let you down. Is that not what we are taught? That people will always fail you. But that same belief has caused people to fail in their own lives because if their neighbor is weak and fallible, how much more are they? Stop believing that you are born clumsy, failure prone, and undependable. That is a scapegoat that has defaulted on its credit. Even those of us that are born with disabilities still prove that one disadvantage does not impede perfection. The light that proceeds from them appears to be even more bright because they are humbled and one with their perfection. They are not accepting that they cannot be responsible because of some deficiency.

Have you realized your responsibility to your neighbor? I hear many of us speak about, "loving our neighbor", but do we really protect each other? We are responsible for the safety of those that dwell amongst us. Promoting selfless acts towards others, especially those adjacent to you, teaches them to reciprocate the act. We must accept our duties to aid our neighbors. We will feel more secure when we protect those that our concern is invested with. If we would emulate this principle, neighbor for neighbor, then all of our natural boundaries would be safe. If we desire for the inside of our homes to be safe, then we must make sure that outside of them are secure as well. Understand that the problem outside of your household will eventually begin to infect the inside. Four walls will not shield you from every danger.

PROVERBS 24:11-12

"If thou forbear to deliver them that are

29

drawn unto death, and those that are ready to
be slain;

If thou sayest, Behold, we knew it not; doth
not he that pondereth the heart consider it?
And he that keepeth thy soul doth not He
know it? And shall not he render to every
man according to his works?"

If you see the bad things and do nothing, your guilt is just as great.

LEVITICUS 5:1

"If a person sins in hearing the utterance of
an oath, and is a witness, whether he has
seen or known of the matter- if he does not
tell it, he bears guilt."

Interact with those that need your assistance and understand their
plight. Protect your family by protecting the families around you.
This only requires a little more compassion, a little more interest in
the whole in which you are a part. Tragedies can be avoided if we
all participate. Children will not disappear into the shadows of
isolation if only we look at them. Hostile fanatics will have no
room to incubate if we surround them with love. All that is asked is
that we care a little bit more.

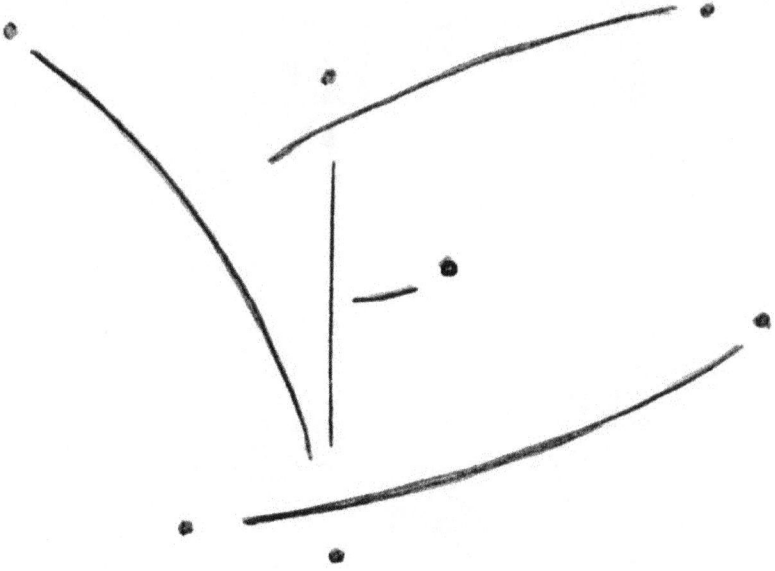

FIVE

POINTS OF A STAR

JUSTICE

SALVATION

FINGERS

CHAPTER 5   YOUR PRISON

Prison. Is it simply a place to punish those that break the law? Those undesirable people that just don't seem to fit in with the rest of the world? Of course! Who else could be designed for such a place? You would never go to prison nor entertain the idea of breaking the law. But although you are not physically constrained, are you actually free? I'm not talking about government oppression or some other sort of physical binding. I mean, what is harboring you from being able to enjoy your life. What makes living so grim and difficult for you? That is your prison and it is more tyrannical than any physical "house" that you could be lodged in. Prison is not just some tangible containment that separates you as a punishment, it is also a subconscious block that impedes your happiness and shatters your faith in people and the Divine. But unlike a physical prison in which someone else is in control, you are the prisoner and guard within your cell block. Whether you believe in Satan or circumstances, you allow it room to maneuver and hold to you.

We immerse ourselves daily in many things without paying much attention to their effects upon us. It is difficult to be positive in a cesspool of violence, horrible ideals, and malicious tones, which is why people are allowed to make terrible decisions so easily. But environment is not the only factor in decision making and cannot be allowed to guide our lives.

Why have you allowed yourself to become trapped? When you cannot "live" without certain objects, you are a prisoner to it. Just as an addict is lost in the world of their high, so too can you become trapped within the false impression that is someone else's dream. How? Well, we are a nation that says that we are opinionated and free to express that opinion but when the majority does not like something that is whom decides what is true/right and what is not. The tide of the world is upset and people become angry but when you ask someone to define what it is that they want, they have no idea. Take the general ideas of the nation. People say that "the government is crooked" or "I hate corporations", but these unifying hymns simply cloud the minds of a great deal of people. Because if you ask for specificity, people really don't know. That is a real problem. Uninformed as to the true bandits in our midst. We are smarter than that. We are more evolved than to suckle down and regurgitate ideas that have long since lost their validity or strength. To spark yourself and become free from this personal yoke, you must clear your thoughts of biased ideas and feelings. Becoming a little judge will allow you to take a position that is different from your original. You will be more dispassionate in your judgment of things thus allowing a clear opinion.

PROVERBS 22:24-25

"Do not become friends with an angry man,
Do not go with him that is furious, "

"lest you learn his ways, and your soul
becomes ensnared."

Anger and hatred are two of the easiest ways of entrapment. We are upset when the day does not begin the way that we want. We are enraged when someone doesn't do what we want. We are furious when we feel as though we are deserving of something and we don't receive it. That is the trap. We are pulled in by our desires and with so much invested; it feels like the stock plummets when we don't make a profit. Walking around with the key to your cell (mind) is difficult. You don't know whether to open it or keep it closed, for protection. You are in fact, your own jailer. You are trapped by your own deceptive thoughts and betray yourself.

Slavish thinking is not a new concept nor was it born with the African Slave trade. Humans continuously become enslaved to outside forces by little measures. Things not respected can creep upon us -unawares.

Men especially have a difficult time with releasing that boiling pressure that infects us. It's appearance is seen as weak if it is expressed any other way than violence. There is a wave of anger flowing through this country. It is almost as if we have regressed into an animalistic stage in this post-industrial age. We allow ourselves to become ensnared by things that really are not even pertinent to our progress but our pride holds a terrible grip. We are persuaded by our irrational thoughts and the more that we mull them over, the more outlandish they become. We all do it. We may become so trapped that anything projected will be logical. You become a prisoner of your own imagination. Anger has a very harsh grip. None of us can defeat it on our own. Prayer, meditation, and good conversation are three ways to step outside of that prison cell.

A physical prison is compiled of order and chaos. A paradox? No not really. See rules are set to allow order to flow throughout a prison (or any infrastructure). To keep conflict within a system down and people safe. The problem is, human boredom and agitation will not allow order to permeate throughout so long.

Imagine in your mind being surrounded by 200 plus individuals all day, every day. There is a torrent of noise that wafts throughout the building that you are confined to. Now, see yourself sharing a room with a person that continues to talk all day about things that neither concern nor affend you. Think of the most irritating conversations that would antagonize you. Whether it may be, visualize this person continuously talking to you about this over and over, seemingly to repeat themselves in a narcissistic tone. The arrogance coming with every breath, the lies, and the incredible sound of confidence. As days go on, being trapped with this conflicting individual could cause you to snap. That is exactly how you feel when you allow other influences to trap your mind. It keeps nagging at you, building support by getting louder, looking for other recipients to support its case. You must take courage to stand and say (declare) enough. Believing in the power of the mind and spirit will allot you the authority to subdue this enemy. Wrestling with your mind is not easy but you must get control or the other occupant will.

Remember that a prison has a purpose. It is designed to lock away those that are not in alignment with society. Those that choose to disobey. Do not lock away yourself in your own mind. It does happen.

SIX

POINTS OF A STAR

OVERPLUS OF THE AMOUNT

(BECAUSE THERE ARE ONLY FIVE
FINGERS)

CHAPTER 6 PERSPECTIVE

We all have our own personal perspectives about life, God, family, just everything in our midst. But who defines (or molded) your perspective? All of our ideals and standards are influenced by our cultures and interactions but are the beliefs that you hold in conflict with your consciousness? Some ideas are so natural, so non-controversial, that they are innately tacituous. Who has positioned the thoughts in your mind? Are they yours or another's? Look at one of the most expressive forms of thought-words. They can be encouraging (good job) or they can be very destructive (I hate you). They hold so much control because they are an arrangement of real energy. They are a force. No matter how sloppily prepared that they are placed; the arranger can produce an efficacy in which they are seeking. So how has someone else's words formed your perspective in this world? Many of us grew up pledging our allegiance to the flag of the United States, even though we had no idea what that meant. Our families influence our beliefs until we reach an age (or stage) of awakening. We begin to ask questions, rebel, and search for answers outside of the nest. Look at Americans. We are taught to believe in freedom and Democracy, but is our concept of freedom the same as someone in China? That, to me, is like the chicken and the egg question. Which came first? I believe that the chicken came first. Why? Because the egg was designed from a reproductive position. All living things were designed with a purpose of reproducing the image for their survival. The reproductor precedes the reproduction. The reproductor is the perfect form of elements and the seed continues to replicate itself perfectly. This is my per-spective through my experience. We all are individualized in our perspectives no matter how bad the idea may be. Our perspectives are built as we live, grow, and internalize those things around us and within us. As we grow, our ideas change but our understanding progresses. Time moves faster, things are not so certain, and problems are more complex and near.

But this is all within your parameters of reality. The things that bother you, bother you. Everyone does not understand the severity of suffering nor can everyone recognize racism from someone who simply does not know or like you. Our perspectives can get out of view when we allow stereotypes to guide our principles. Blacks hate Mexicans, Mexicans hate whites, all whites are racists. We are full of these ideas because they are allowed to run around without contestation. We are eventually immersed with toxic ideas because they are not challenged.

Silently introspect and discover your view of life. What is it that you see? Don't depend on what someone else has molded in you but really become aware of life in and around you. Are the people that you thought to be enemies truly so or has someone else's hatred formed your view? Does your faith really ask you to hate? When you pray or meditate, do you feel a surreal calm, peace? That is when your perspective is clear. That is when you block out all of the piercing noise and listen to the echo that moves throughout all life. The truth about life is not hidden. It is not secluded within some lost cave. It is within you but you seem to be the only one that does not see it. God used to admonish the Israelites with a simple saying: SHMAH and it simply means "Listen, hear, obey". Now it is time for you to listen, hear, and obey. Make sure that you do not miss the call.

SEVEN

COMPLETION

PERFECTION

HEAVENS

OATH

VOW

N. Malaki Crayton

CHAPTER 7   SUFFERING

When we think of suffering, we immediately think of pain or some intolerable affliction. But it is more about the ability to endure these events that allow us to appreciate more. Suffering is seen as a menacing plight caused by men. It is not seen as a universal part of the whole. Think about when you have had a terrible headache. Remember how bad that you felt as you endured it. Now if you took some sort of aspirin or other remedy, think about how uplifted you felt when relief came. That suffering, that endurance made you so much more appreciative. Sadly, the next day, you forgot about the pain and the release from it. This same tragedy happens in many aspects of our lives. Look at our perspective (respect) to death. We are afraid and loathe it. Why? Because of our selfish desire to live "our lives". So we attempt to do things that will thwart death. Even our religious beliefs comfort us as they offer a safe-haven (security) against our design. Eternal life in bliss, our own little retirement bonus for doing an outstanding job at work. But think about it. Death and life (at least in this world) are intertwined. When a volcano erupts, it destroys everything in its path but in doing so, it expands the canvas of the land and soon provides new growth of trees and flowers. When animals and plants die, their bodies (and ours) decompose and return back into the land providing nutrients for the soil, which none of us could survive without. We are always upset when tragedies happen or when someone close to us dies "unexpectedly". These are not haphazard events. These tragedies force us to look upon one another with more sincerity and compassion. They reveal the humility that all of us possess but are afraid to share.

When someone dies, we "hold in" our feelings. We are told not to grieve naturally and in fact hurt ourselves as we harbor this burden. You cannot hold in the death of another. It is dishonorable and selfish. How can anyone know how great that person was if not expressed through you. You must share their greatness with others. This will also relieve you of the pain of their transformation. Do not grieve in isolation or private. This only makes you more resistant to loving those that require your full presence. That is selfish. That is idol suffering. Release yourself from the restriction of selfish suffering and recognize the spiritual balance in all physical entities.

Job (Bible) even emphasizes it when he says, "Shall we accept good from God, and shall not accept adversity?" (Job 2:10). Our adversarial components must be matched by our loving camaraderie. Our pain is only allowed to advance as far as we accept adversity alone. To persevere through the emotion that is pain, we must accept its reality and subdue its effect. Suffering, on an intimate level, requires one to recognize God's active position in everything around them and to be more receptive to compassion as it is given by those that care. Suffering, on a massive stage, needs a community of shared spirits funneled together to act with purpose to confront it head on.

EIGHT

INFINITY

DOUBLE CONSTANT

LOOP

CHAPTER 8   THE TRUTH

Why is it that some people can believe so fervently in an idea and call it truth? This is not exclusive to one religious sect or class of people. This, as HISTORY displays, is spread across a spectrum of time and geography. But really ask yourself, "What makes something true?" Some will say that the Bible is true because it is authoritative of God's expression to man. But a billion Muslims will say the same about the Qu'ran. Some of us will defer to "facts" because they have been tested and proven. We seem to be so certain of things in this world that we sometimes even deceive our own minds with admonished lies.

Truth (in Hebrew) is rooted in stability which means that truth stems from comfort and assurance. When we are comfortable, our blood pressure is leveled, our nerves are not acting erratically, and our thoughts are not plagued by inconsistencies. Truth has the same effect. It frees you from the burden of uncertainty. Now, that is not to say that there are not things that we are uncertain of but it unlocks the yoke of stress and fear because you understand that all of these are factors that will only do as much damage as you allow them to do. Stop believing in the inconsistencies of your past by allowing them to set the foundation for your future.

Truth is built. It is affirmed, not so much in our ability to believe in it, but in its persistence to be consistent, unwavering, and evolving in its nature. It proves itself through loyalty. Truth is not patented by anyone nor have any of us authored it. It was here before us and it will always be present, even if the world were to end. Jesus said," Do not think that I came to destroy the law or the prophets. I did not come to destroy but to fulfill. (18). For assuredly I say to thee, till heaven and earth pass away, one jot or one tittle will by no means pass from the law till all is fulfilled." (Matthew 5:17-18). I know that the earth is still here, and I don't see heaven leaving if the earth hasn't, so why would I think that Truth has dissipated.

We must stop being blind hopefuls. Believing in the Divine does not mean doing so because someone told you to. No one can answer for your crimes/sins/iniquity. Paul tells you, "...work out your own salvation with fear and trembling." (Philippians 2:12). Everything in the universe appears to have a failsafe. It has its protocol. Truth is revealed in every aspect of life at every interval. We just have to pay attention.

NINE

SYSTEMS IN THE BODY

CHAPTER 9   THE BALANCE

There is one underlying balance in all of the principles in this world. Whatever grammatical surgeries that our languages may take or new understandings in science, spiritual principles do not change. Spiritual laws do not dissipate because we do not believe in them. They are as stationary as the foundations of the earth. The same continuing design that was set forth in the beginning of creation is present in us and our everyday achievements.

Just because there are flaws within all religious sects does not mean that the experience of God is absent in our lives. Today, we ridicule those that claim to speak to God or that they are of God, yet we believe so fervently in those stories written and passed down that speak of men and women interacting with God, and in one known story, God becoming a man. We are not aware of how much the infinite spirit works, nor how prophets are chosen, so who are we to declare that there is no communication between man and his Creator. God is not absent in our lives, nor does It require your fear to exist. God requires our respect and obedience. When you are in fear of something, you do not trust it. You are seeking a way to outwit it. There is a reluctant desire to be loyal because how could you trust something that you believed was going to hurt you for a mistake or a mishap. Fear enables resistance. I would hope that you would not fear God in the hidden sense, but respect the Divine and believe in the Truth of your connection to it. Live as it has designed you to live.

What do you believe? Do you believe that Abraham, Moses, Jesus or anyone that has brought a message to save people, taught it with maliciousness or hatred? These messages are not filled with prejudicial animosity. It is only our ability to give power to those that are hateful that allows for evil messages to be passed on. Everything on this planet has the desire to survive. Every being is ingrained with qualities of preservation, but as humans, we mustn't enforce our will to the point of extermination. We are not the owners of this planet but guardians (custodians). It is scintillating how quickly we are to destroy one another. It is as if we are bound to suicide subconsciously. To others, it looks as though we hate each other for everything and fight one another for anything.

Good and evil do not grow out of the earth. They are positions that we either choose to act on or not. Either way, these acts are done (committed to) by us. There are zealous people in every religious sect that are unhappy. You see who they are. Everyone else is the enemy. Everyone else is going to be punished by some terrible event. Maybe you are one of them. The yoke that they are bound by will not appease the people in their midst. I believe in the power of choice. The balance between the idea and the manifestation of that idea. God had an idea and we are the application of that idea. Men have made chains where God simply made order.

Create and imaginate are intertwined in Biblical usage. The interdependency of the spiritual and physical are evident in the beginning. If you sit and absorb the wind as it breezes pass, you can feel the connection between you and all other living things. Allowing the mind to connect with that feeling is like tapping into the spirit of the earth and the Divine.

People require joy to live. People must realize that joy implies a closer connection to the Divine. God is our joy and is in all living beings, which is why interacting with other people is critical.

Happiness comes from within but it is re-enforced through interactive relationships. Ever notice how someone can change the mood of the crowd? How easily certain people in your life can make you happy as soon as they come into your presence? That is the connection. That is the balance. That is the presence of the Divine being fulfilled in you.

Recognizing the balance in life means that you should never become overly complacent with anything. All things possess the ability to change whether they are social, physical, or financial. Everything seen and unseen, is in constant motion and stability. There will always be active forces that change things while allowing the character of the entity to remain. Ice will always be water. Diamonds will always be carbon. Humans will always be God-like and earth-like.

Sometimes we become too attached to things and are not able to tolerate its change. But the stability comes in that it's change may be necessary to benefit whatever is directly involved with it. We learn in school that we cannot create nor destroy mass, matter, or energy. What we really do is borrow it. Heat and energy are transferred from other entities into us and we utilize this to improve our lives. That is stability in motion. That is balance in action.

Arrogance is a blindfold for spiritual recklessness. We must eliminate the dividing thought, the depraved ridicule, and the eyes of malice. These things that we conjure up or allow to invade our minds unnecessarily offset our balance. Satan, the devil, or whatever name that you choose to call the negative influence of this world has only the authority that you permit it.

The Divine Creator tells you;

GENESIS 4:6-7

> "So the Lord sayeth to Cain, "Why are you angry? And why has your face fallen? If you do what is right will you not be accepted? And if you do what is not right, sin couches at your door, and its desire is for you, but you can master it."

PROVERBS 10:9

> "He who walks with integrity, walks securely."

The terrible things that pervert our minds can be controlled. Don't let them in. Let us look at one of those spears: ANGER. We must not be lured into the sensation of it so easily. It makes us unpredictable to ourselves. Relying on it to protect us in times of uncertainty is reckless and dangerous. We mustn't use it to strengthen us when we are hurt because it only encourages it more. It is a poison that spreads and devours everything. It makes us see things that do not exist and allows us to justify things that are not true.

Extreme polarizing ideas also must not be permitted to define the application of our character. The balance is about inner and outer equilibrium. It is the manifestation of your spiritual balance in reality around you. The person that we reveal daily is directly connected to the essence that is your spirit. Whether we mask it in an illusionary character or over expose ourselves, it will always be revealed at some junction. If your connection has no stability, then your character will show its weaknesses through constant uncertainty in your actions.

When we allow ourselves to understand the position of others, we are more effective human beings, and when we understand ourselves, we are more receptive to the world around us. Our design is that of a social, interactive, and emotionally charged nature. Continue to be human and you will continue to be balanced.

N. Malaki Crayton

PART II   THE IMAGE

N. Malaki Crayton

TEN
(FOCUS ON THE 0)

WHOLE

CONSTANT

360 DEGREES

CHAPTER 10   PERFECTION

I believe that who you are regulates what you will do, but what you do continues to refine who you are. When you allow yourself to be influenced by the Divine, you incur natural inhibitors that will impede you from going over the edge. All humans hold the possibility to do horrible things, yet we choose not to do bad things because of fear, respect, love, or courtesy. These are ideals that reveal who we are. These attributes protect us from becoming out-of-control.

You do not believe in Perfection? Well, you should because you are surrounded by it and made from it. The earth is perfect. It does what it was designed to do. With its many variables and "catastrophes: it continues to sustain life. God is perfect, isn't he? Luke tells us in verse 21, "nor will they say, lo here! or lo there! For indeed, the Kingdom of God is within you." And God breathed the Breath of Life into us. If Gods Spirit dwells in us, why is perfection so difficult to accept? Your Creator designed you to be perfect, a complete being. What was one of the most specific commandments that God gave to Abraham? "Walk thou before me and be thou Perfect" (Genesis 17:1). I believe that Jesus said something similar, "Be ye perfect as your Father in Heaven is perfect", (Matthew 5:48).

I Corinthians 3:16

> "Do you not know that you are the temple of
> God and that the Spirit of God dwells in
> you? If anyone defiles the temple of God,

God will destroy him. For the temple of God
is Holy, which temple ye are."

What is the problem with us believing in perfection? We have
changed the standard, the understanding that defines perfection in
the perfect design. You were created by a perfect being, with a perfect idea, and formed from a perfect substance. Energy and matter
cannot be destroyed nor do we possess the ability to make it either.
Science class right? That's right! We are able to work, think, and
act. It will, of course, be returned upon the day of our expiration as
promised by our Creator.

Genesis 3:19

> "In the sweat upon your brow you shall eat
> bread till you return to the ground, For out
> of it you were taken; For dust you are, And
> to dust you shall return."

Ecclesiastes 3:19, 20

> For what happens to the sons of men also
> happens to beasts; one thing befalls them: as
> one dies, so dies the other. Surely they all
> have one breath: man has no advantage over
> beasts, for all is vanity.

> All go to one place: all are from the dust,
> and all return to the dust.

We are in fact borrowed mass and energy. Our Creator simply
molded us out of mass and energy that was already existent.

We have lost the idea of real perfection, which impedes our connection with the Divine. Our natural instructions are simply to

ALIGN US WITH our source thus revealing our perfection in completion (Spirit, elements, function).

What are some of the qualities that express our perfection? Besides our natural abilities to adapt and evolve, our differences make us all perfect. Humans, no matter what hue, culture, or country, can reproduce an offspring with a different partner. We are genetically built to survive no matter our ideological beliefs. We allow our prejudicial barriers (race, language, tradition, class, economic status) to impede us in this world.

There are no exceptions when it concerns people. The Divine has blessed all with an ability to tap into the Universal Intelligence. Although we are different, we are not separate. Our differences are not as vast as our commonalities. We share the same air, water, energy, and design in structure, likes and dislikes. Energy is something that we all feel and need and it is moved around and passed through objects, so too can our emotions be passed from being to being. We are told that Love is the Bond of Perfection (Colossians). Jesus speaks of perfection on many occasions but one in particular moves me;

Matthew 19:21

> "Jesus said to him, "If you want to be perfect, go, sell what you have and give to the poor, and you will have treasure in heaven; and come, follow me."

I don't necessarily believe that he wants you to be poor, but more so alleviating yourself of the distraction of wealth. Warren Buffett, Bill Gate, and Melinda Gates are three of the wealthiest people on the planet, not simply because they give away billions of dollars, but because they are not distracted by the wealth or the allotment of it. They actually are sincere about the people that they are involved with and this allows them to be effective in the world. The bond of Love that is the key to perfection. Recognizing the Divine Equilibrium in the world and acting on it with sincerity.

Servitude produces a perfect balance. There is no perfection without service. Our interactive behavior requires that we perform service to one another selflessly.

Perfection has been twisted by ideological disputes and deception. Many people equate perfection with beauty. If you are not pretty then you are not perfect. The lascivious eye. Every being is beautiful in the eyes of the Creator. Everyone is attractive to someone in the world as we are all designed to pair up. Our perfection is seen when we perform our duties as humans. When seasons change and plants disappear and rise again. When musicians inspire us to feel happier about ourselves. When mothers (working or stay-at-home) raise, nurture, and love their children, all express the act of perfection.

Our children are so caught up in a tragic perception of perfection that they are literally killing themselves over flaws. Children are susceptible to bullying because adults allow ridiculous ideas of success, beauty, and popularity to run rampant. We are intrigued by the latest fads and outrageous acts. We praise people in television for their rude and anarchical behavior because we believe in freedom (we also like seeing others act as fools). Freedom is not a credit card. It is not some pass for bad behavior.

Children are vulnerable to bad images because we create the atmosphere for it. We mustn't allow others perception of perfection to invade and distort our lives.

We allow too many things to tell us if we are worthy or not. Many of us today are trapped by stuff. The more options that we have, the more entrenched we become. Some don't even realize the depth in which they have become immersed. Are you someone that has voluntarily placed a yoke around your neck? Do you feel as though you are suffocating because you can't obtain enough items to make you happy? Be careful because it does become an addiction and you will become lost in any addiction.

You must recognize the perfection that already exists within you and around you. Look at the "flaws" and see how they make you unique. These "flaws" allow us to be interested in others. Different things attract you. The same bores you. Things are not dull because we have a world full of differences.

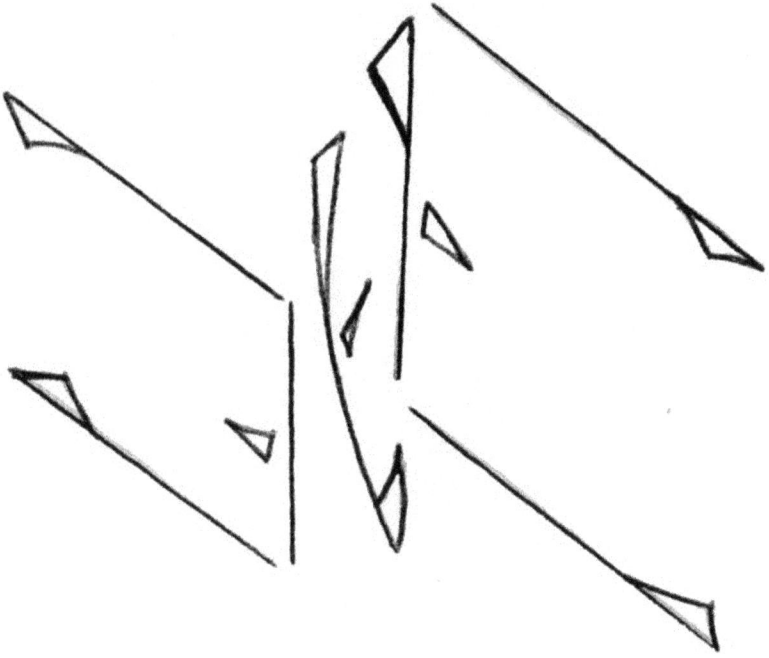

ELEVEN

EXPRESS YOUR UNIQUENESS IN
UNITY

CHAPTER 11 YETZER

Everything in this universe began with an Idea (or from an idea). All things are invoked from the imagination of the Creator and everything that we invent is a derivative from the Creators imprint upon us. When the world was formed in the book of Genesis, the word Bara' is used which is consistent with molding something. Yetzer is more of an intimate connection. With this word imagination and create are intertwined. It means that the Creator took a part of itself and imprinted in us. The innovation required to make something requires a reflected part of its maker which is why this word is even pertinent to our survival.

We are a creation out of the imagination of God. We must recognize God's presence within everything around us and see how we are connected in a way that permits us an advantage. Our imaginations must be nurtured and invoked with inspiration. Our bodies are filled with natural energy. This energy powers the neurons in our bodies. We are filled with the same energy that vibrates throughout the universe. Ever notice how you can get excited over something and get chill bumps? Pay attention to how a crowd reacts at games and they become overwhelmed with euphoria. That is a connecting joy. That is experiencing a link similar to the spirit. That connection, all on the same wavelength, fills everyone and sparks that feeling that makes everyone happy to be alive. That is an example of the touch of life being expressed through being. When you are appreciative for that Divine energy, it will secure you even in the harshest environments.

This imaginative thought to create is innate in every being. It must be nurtured and fed. We cannot sit around allowing it to dissipate. Your potential to create happiness in your life and those around you lies in your ability to be content with your inner being. Just as "evil devices" can be conjured up, so can good plans be utilized to impede those. But you must focus in and mold those ideas into reality. How much do you procrastinate? How reluctant are you to manifest your ideas because you don't believe that they are worthy of fruition? We must recognize that we are sagacious beings that were designed by an intelligent Creator in whom we are to emulate.

The power to create is only limited by our desire to bring these ideas out of us. We block our own possibilities by reluctant action from fear either of success or ridicule.

Imaginative thought must be given a positive direction in order to carry its host into genuine action. Our imaginations are so powerful a tool in our existence that our perceptions can be altered by it. Never, ever, forget that everything in and around you came from an idea. I think that because we are so acclimated with everything in our midst that we have lost the excitement of the innovation behind these inventions. Think of how our ancestors must have viewed the world without all of our discoveries. Do you get excited about electricity? What about airplanes? Or what about toilet paper? No. Exactly what I mean. Nobody is awestruck by these things because they are a natural part of our everyday life. Think of what could be a part of our everyday existence tomorrow.

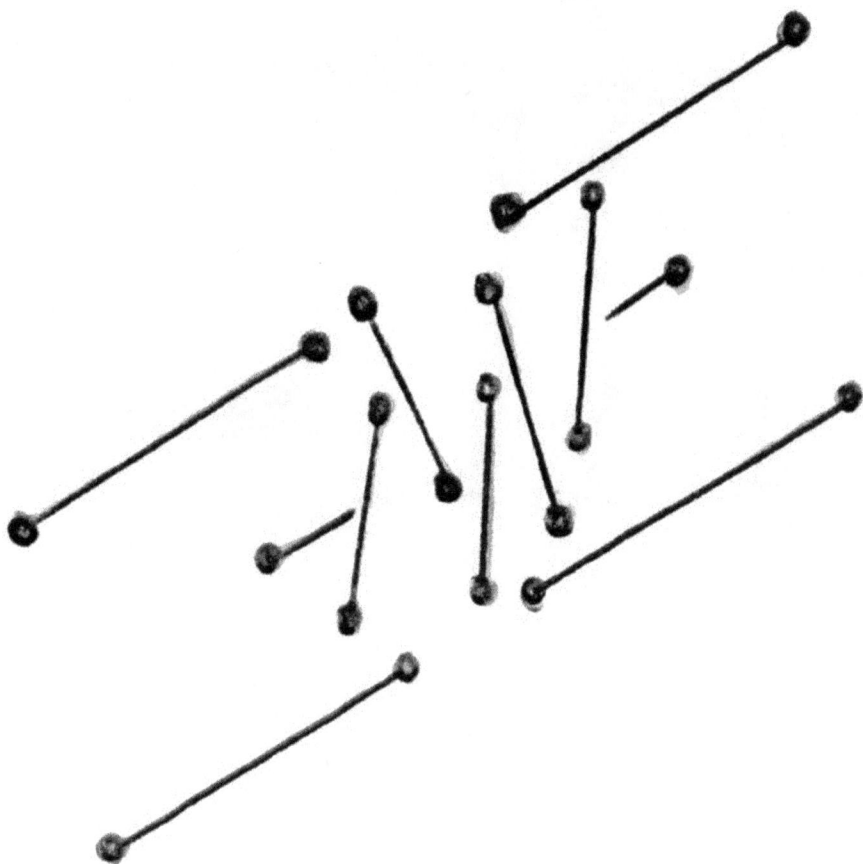

TWELVE

CHARACTERS ARE REVEALED OVER
TIME AND CIRCUMSTANCES,

TRUST IN YOURS.

N. Malaki Crayton

CHAPTER 12 CHARACTER

A person's character is the first thing that is revealed in any engagement. When you first encounter someone, you take in their body language, speech, eyes, confidence (or lack thereof), and that eery or comfortable spirit that you feel while talking to them. Characters are revealed over time and circumstances. People think that it does not change and would like for it to remain consistent and unwavering but most times this is simply not how it works, unless you're a socio-path. You don't do the things that you did in your youth and you are not the same as you were in high school or even college. The core fabric of a person's being may remain (who I define myself as) but the expression (how do I speak and interact with the world) will almost certainly change. All humans either upgrade or downgrade, but you will change. The problem comes in that we don't always like the change. We don't enjoy having to readapt to something new when something old is easily understood. As we process more information, we make new discoveries, innovate new technology, and extrapolate new pieces of our world. Thus, who we are must change with the coming environment.

Humans have only survived in this world, this long, with so many enemies (poisons, droughts, cancers, extreme weather) because our Creator designed us with the unique ability to learn and grow. In every way, we maintain the gift of adaptation. Our characters, which are our chosen expression in the world, must grow as well. When you are young, you are certain about everything. When you grow and experience, you begin to ask questions. When you mature and live, you see the Divine in all life.

Some of us are taught to hate and others adopt it for personal animosities. The thing is though, it doesn't last. Some people's characters expressed hatred of others for years and as what happens with all life, the world changes. That era of expressive hate will only last as long as that person chooses to hang on to a false identity. The true expressive form of the spirit does not make you angry or bitter. Think about it like this. The Spirit that enlivens everything must be filled with pure energy because everything in this universe functions off of energy. So, when you get a boost of energy (caffeine, sugar, happy feelings, encouragement) how do you feel? Alive and great, friendly. That exact same euphoria is created by a true, genuine connection with the spirit that allows you to execute a positive expression in physical form. That is the true testament of character. That is what humans respect. That is what we must seek if we are to truly be unified.

Ask yourself (yes it's okay to ask), who am I? What do I believe? Do I like what I believe or are they someone else's perspectives? Do I care more about the way that I look, think, or act?

There are many times when we may not like the answers that we get but you must appreciate what you discover. Look, if you don't know who you are then no one else will either. Think about it. You don't like confusion, so why would anyone else like it? There are no good solutions found in chaos. Make sure that you obtain stability in your expedition.

If you read the Bible, Qu'ran, the Tao, spirituality, they all hold standards in which you should conduct yourself. There are rules in every culture that defines that identity from another. But while the identity of the world's cultures may differ, the humanistic detail is always constant:

1. There is a greater Being that created us.

2. Love your brother and sister.

3. Don't harm others.

4. Protect your family.

5. Help others that require your assistance.

These principles are imprinted upon us naturally. We know when actions are not appropriate because they stain our character. They degrade the energy that flows through us that we express. Humans are very active. As hypocritical as it appears, as much as we dislike change, consistency bores us after some time. This is why the character must evolve or depreciate. I remember reading a story about a great thinker and he changed his position on an issue and someone labeled him a hypocrite and he responded, "When I find that I am wrong, I correct myself. What do you do?" This is our great economist John Maynard Keynes. That is evolution. That is a growing spirit. That is a character that upgrades itself to continue growing. We must continue to review and correct ourselves as we grow. This is required maintenance on our part.

THIRTEEN

ARROGANCE IS A BLINDFOLD FOR
RECKLESSNESS

CHAPTER 13   EVOLVING BARBARISM

Are we more or less civil than our ancestors? Although originally the term barbaric was used for those unwilling to accept the new religion, its modern usage is seen as those without morals or manners. It is given to people that we view as having less civil qualities than those of us living in this democracy. But with devastating crime waves, governments worldwide viewed as the apparatus of evil on earth, and reputable people being exposed as fraudulent, how far have we really excelled from 2,000 years ago?

This world has become so modernized with technology, our living arrangements, interactions, and relationships are better yet there are still things that we wrestle to change with. On a global scene, many of us appear to be civil, but internally we all still harbor whispers of old problems. Women are still blanketed as inferior, hue still plays some part in our views to one another (on all sides), and arrogance continues to fill us until we explode and crash. Religious and spiritual interpretations are still used as manipulating and oppressive devices. Politics, in no era, have ever been fully transparent or without depravity. Humans at every level seem to give in to lascivious actions. We are what we are but the application of our intellect defines who we are.

Our laws are a combination of preventive measures and committed atrocities in which we hope to deter and overcome. So, why is it that we continuously have high crime and violence, not just in America, but the world over? Be realistic. There has always been an intolerant amount of violence and anarchy but through technology, it is no longer hidden. We become sickened by the scenes displayed on T.V. of children maurdered, raped, and abused.

The horror of an entire town being eradicated is shocking. We are even provoked to act when natural catastrophes happen. But even in all of this, terrible events continue to arise. How could a loving God continue to allow such things? You know what, the horridity of human depravity has always been blamed on everything else but the vehicle in which it is revealed: US.

We have been desensitized to the evil right in our midst for so long that it appears unreal. These terrible people don't just pop up and decide to do evil, it is nurtured and molded. It has its inception and is cultivated by its host.

The nature in which we allow wretched acts to penetrate our societies is accomplished by our ability to ignore these horrors. We don't believe that these events affect us because they are not adjacent to us but always remember that just as light and sound are reflected across the universe, so too are evil agendas bounced around and absorbed. There needn't be a multitude of like minded people for an idea to become cultivated. As long as there is one vessel that harbors an idea, it will always be, but as long as there is another there to challenge this, it can be contained.

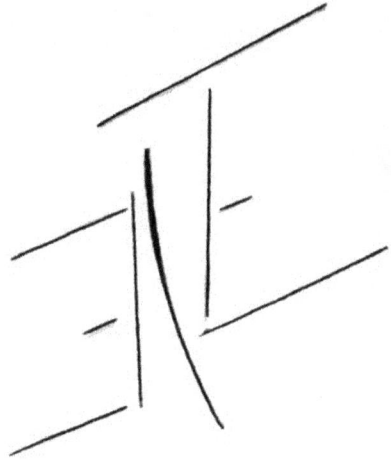

FOURTEEN

ONE PEOPLE, ONE LANGUAGE, ONE STANDARD:

LOVE

N. Malaki Crayton

CHAPTER 14   EVOLVING STABILITY

We are solidified with a common purpose,
a subconscious solidarity that allows us to evolve together.

A great deal of people don't like to use the word evolve because it seems to take credit away from the Creator of life. Many see it as outright blasphemy or disrespect to the Divine but I do not believe that our designer limited our ability to grow. If we did not adapt socially, academically, interactively, mentally, physically, then we would not survive in this world. Our bodies are injected with small viruses to allow the immune system to build up immunity, the body must shock the old muscle to build up new muscle, and the mind must challenge itself if it is to expand its scope.

Our experience and improvement grows from generation to generation. Fear can never outmaneuver love and so it cannot be a formidable impediment to aiding each other. That is our binding strength when we assist one another which in return aids us on many levels. People persevere, humanity improves because of our innate ability to adapt and push forward. The possibility of things going awry is always present (and sometimes persistent) but this does not allot us the excuse to give up. We mustn't give leverage to those things that have the potential to destroy us. Too many of us put locks on inanimate objects that if lost, will evoke emotional distractions within us.

Our language must be terse and without manipulative error.

Recognize that fluctuating decisions and feelings will always cause disruptive actions. The senseless depravity that invades this world through human opportunity is astounding. We approach evilness as a thing, as some sort of mythical creature that appears and hides as it finds entry to wreak chaos upon us. We must never forget that those that commit horrible acts are diligent and are never at calm unless they have done something terrible daily. They must feed that craving as any other addiction requires as appetite. We must be just as diligent in our effectiveness because at base, it is a war of applied ideas.

FIFTEEN

COMMAND YOUR SPEECH.

IT IS YOUR MOST POWERFUL
CONNECTIVE WEAPON.

CHAPTER 15   TO SPEAK

Speaking is so powerful an apparatus that some of us seem to forget just how magnetic that it is. Controlling (commanding) your speech is simply about the proper arrangement of its content. Words are appointed and arranged a certain position in order to manipulate a result. Your result. How effective do you desire the message to be and what kind of receptiveness are you looking for. Speaking is rooted in arranging a message. To make communication between two entities understood. That is its purpose and goal.

Why is language so powerful? Because words can move millions or they can cause one to move a million. Words manipulate, irritate, or illuminate. We must be conscientious in which way that we display our ideas because they can be easily misinterpreted.

Speech is very potent when it comes to influence. It is probably one of the most powerful tools when dealing with people. Take a look at the book of Genesis. In chapter 1, God said, "Let there be light", and there was light. Whether you take this in the literal sense or an allegorical perspective, God spoke and an action followed. How comfortably shocking this idea is. The Hebrew word Amar' is used here, more accurately is seen as "to declare or say". God declared something and it became. We do this on a smaller level when we tell someone our name. We are declaring what our existence will be recognized as and what we expect others to see in us. When we tell our children that they cannot go outside until they have completed a task, we have declared a rule by manifesting it verbally. We have set the standard. We have, in essence, brought it into existence. The power of speech is not so difficult to grasp because we are all subject to it.

Words are an intangible force that can be mastered. When Jesus proclaimed, "Peace be still", there was calm. When we recognize that the power within these words is influential and penetrating, we begin to see how easy it is for people to become manipulated. People do not believe that music holds manipulative potential. Really? So your mood has never been swayed by the type of music that you've listened to? True, it may not have had you act on your emotional involvement but I know that it definitely encouraged it. For thousands of years, the sound of beating drums was used to encourage the confidence in its soldiers and place terror in its enemies. The constant thump of the beat would align itself with the beat of the heart and unify the soldiers in spirit.

Now, if this worked for thousands of soldiers, for thousands of years as a tactical move, what more could it do to a teenager with an underdeveloped mind. Enter words with an emotional tie to a struggle or scenario that is kindred to that of the listener and you have a willing vessel that is now a servant to his commanders instructions. Although no one can make you do anything, the multiple factors can be so encouraging that refusing would seem almost insane. How do you think that a 14 year old child can walk up to a crowd and open fire? Why do you think that it is a 10 year old can be made to wear a bomb and blow himself up? Do we classify these children as insane or are they just influenced by a mind that uses persuasive language and tools?

It is now recognized (by experiments and testing) that people under extreme duress will say whatever it is that they are told to say. If something is repeated over and over, they will repeat it back as if it were their own thought. People naturally want to appease, and when the speech used is commanding and persuasive, people will agree to anything.

Speech really can invigorate or destroy. If you tell someone that you love them (or care for them), they feel an additional electrifying connection. You have given them a boost. On the other side, if you say, "I hate you", you have destroyed something within that person. We must be careful in the way that we express ourselves to people because you can literally enliven or kill with it. Think of how effective bullies have been over the last few years. Not just with children but adults as well. We mockingly say, "Oh why would someone kill themself because of what someone else said?", but what we don't know is how much power those words held over that person. You will elect someone because of the clarity in words that they convey over a podium. The judge, with the power of his words, can sentence you to life or death. You, with the power of your words, can expand or terminate anything or anyone in your life. Sometimes we do not screen the thought before it comes out of us which is why we get into conflicts unnecessarily. In considering how the recipient may receive the information will allow us to better the process in which we give it.

N. Malaki Crayton

SIXTEEN

ELIMINATE THE DIVIDING
THOUGHTS THAT RIDICULE US AND
MAKE US FEAR.

CHAPTER 16   POSITION

The position that we hold plays a prominent role in how we are viewed in societies everywhere. Religion, politics, human rights, taxes all are factored ingredients in who we define ourselves to be. Problem is that we fall slaves to things that are not beneficial. Falling in love with inanimate things that cannot reciprocate is dangerous. They cannot protect our inner balance. Money can only protect you as far as those animated beings allow for, and if they are not favorable to you, your money becomes as effective as dust.

Your position must be strongly anchored but appreciably tolerant; because you are positioned a certain way does not mean that everyone in your path is an enemy. You can't be pro-you and anti-everyone else. Your position should not threaten nor become intrusive to others. We all share this planets resources and its space. Everywhere is our home because we are born of the earth's ingredients and to it, we will return.

Our place in this world must be in alignment with life. It cannot be pertinent if it is not to be rewarded with the benefits of love and appreciation to our Creator and our brothers/sisters in creation. Our position is fortified in life with service and interactive behavior. The continuous receptiveness and reproduction of the human code must be nurtured for our stability. The fabric of humanity must persevere, consistent with the succeeding generations of children.

Do not fear God to the point of rejection and avoidance. You must fear losing that connection (to God) more than fearing the existence of your Creator. If you are constantly afraid of a being, then you look at it as a burden to be around. You become resentful as a child placed on punishment. Fearing punishment allows creative representatives to come up with false securities. You must see the Creator as your need. Be dependent on that connection and the fear of losing (displacing/replacing) that will keep you focused. If you love someone and fear losing them, then you will become more humbled and appreciative towards them. Stop looking at the Divine as some angry and jealous man. The Divine Creator created the balance, respects it, and does not discriminate within it.

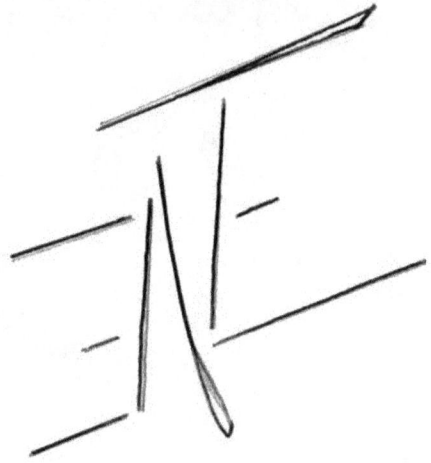

SEVENTEEN

CHAPTER 17 DISGUST AND RECOVERY

ROMANS 1:32

> "Who, knowing the righteous judgment of
> God, that those who practice such things are
> deserving of death, not only do the same but
> also find pleasure in those that do them."

Hypocrisy is not simply limited to those that say and do the opposite but it stretches to those that vicariously do wicked through others. The grip of wicked ideas uses multiple avenues to attack: Anger, lusts, envy, jealousy, selfishness are all connected. They are not separate entities with different agendas; they are interwoven into the objective of your destruction. You may overcome all of these factors but one, and if left unchallenged, will allow a flood of disruption into your midst. This is why it is pivotal to allot discipline from one area to the next, even if you believe that you do not have a threat in this area. Ever seen someone restricted from something for so long that when they come into contact, they have no defense? When you have built no defense then you are not prepared for the enemy that you do not know.

If you are disgusted or defiant at something, let it be the thing that has the ability to trap you. Inanimate objects should never hold power over us but the fallible human condition always permits its entry for these things to happen. Make it your enemy. Look upon it with disgust. Think about how you feel knowing that this object holds this much control over you, how weak you feel in its presence, and how bad you feel when you recognize YOUR subjection to it. Look at bullies. They only have the power to hurt us because we give it to them. Children are not the only ones that face bullies. Their makeup may be different but their tactics are the same. Aggressive, witty, diligent, watchful, sneaky, and they wear masks to hide their monstrous form. But their only true power is in their ability to make us feel bad about our flaws, but that is just it, they are ours and no one else's..

Just as we should not find happiness in the wretched actions of others, we should not applaud when our "enemies" fall. You are not to do as they do or are you no different?

PROVERBS 24:17-18

> "Do not rejoice when thou enemy falleth, and do not let thou heart be glad when he stumbleth,

> Lest the Lord see it, and it displeases him, and he turn away his wrath from him."

PART III   THE DIRECTION

EIGHTEEN

YOUR IDEAS HAVE NO EXPIRATION DATE, REVEAL YOURS

CHAPTER 18   THE IDEA

All things in the universe were sparked by the power of an idea. A thought birthed out of the essence of the Infinite Intelligence. All of the buildings that surround us, all of the weapons that hurt us, and even us, ourselves, began with an idea. There is one central intelligence; one consciousness that links all of us in which we define as God. Our Creator is linked into all of us which also means that we are all hooked into one another. Your feelings and emotions can infect another because that Divine link is connected to all living entities. Sometimes you can finish another person's sentence before they finish or you understand what someone is attempting to say when they cannot say it. These connections are on the same communicating thought path. Even though some of our ideas may be horrible, some of our thoughts malicious, we are all capable of these same thoughts. Humanity is cursed with the power of free "market" thinking. Our thoughts are only regulated by our ability to contain them. You must be the regulator of what you allow to permeate from your mind to the world. When our ideas go sour, what do we do? Come up with better ideas that are more creative than the former. Anything can be changed because although ideas are eternal, they can evolve. Ideas can be moved, shuffled, added to, or contained.

An idea equals perfection. A standard is set with the birth of an idea. We must always remember that ideas put forth will always produce some sort of effect. What kinds of ideas do you have? Do you hope to bring them into this world? You must extract them out of the mind and place them in this reality. Don't take your ideas for granted. Assuming that they are frivolous only means that you don't trust yourself. Everyone questions their ideas. Everyone thinks and re-thinks their thoughts.

The gift of an idea must be appreciated and recognized for its scintillating inception. The inspiration that is bloomed with an idea must be held in order to persevere. Ideas are so common that we overlook its purpose. As with all ideas, they touch our world through consistent application of failures and triumphs. Our successful endeavors prove to us and the world that our ideas are real things. Real energy that can be translated into a more tangible reality. But as long as you covet your ideas and don't release them into reality, you won't build trust within yourself.

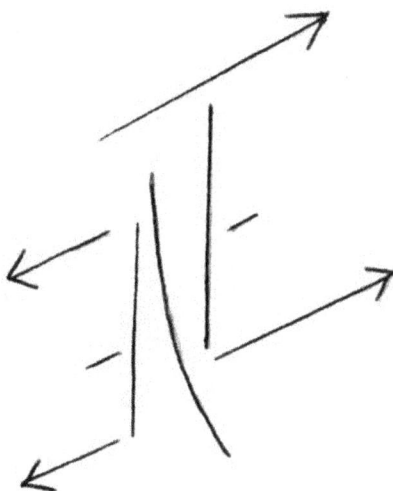

NINETEEN

I BELIEVE IN THE INTELLIGENT,

NOT IN STEREOTYPES.

CHAPTER 19 CERTAINTY AND UNCERTAINTY

Many people seem to be so certain of their place in this world and what they must do. Some have a touch of arrogance, others are reassured with religious doctrine, and yet others still just recognize the parallel harmony in all beings. When you are uncertain, fear, anxiety, and mistakes arise without caveat. Although we think that if you are uncertain of something, you appear weak, it is actually a humbling rod that makes you remember the fragility of your being. We are so certain of everything right up until everything goes wrong. People always seem to blame God when things go awry. Of course we tend to forget that the Divine created all things:

ISAIAH 45:5-7

> "I am the Lord, and there is no other; There is no God besides me. I will gird you, though you have not known me, That they may know from the rising of the sun to its setting, that there is none besides me, I am the Lord, and there is no other: I form the light and create darkness, I make peace and create evil: I, the Lord, do all these things."

PROVERBS 16:4

> "The Lord has made all for Himself, Yea, even the wicked for the day of doom."

Certainty usually arises from repetition, experience, or study.

People believe that they are certain of things that they are exceptional at. Those things that are proven permit us this certainty. But what of those things inexperienced or unseen? We are afraid of the events that occur without preparation. Arrogance is an infectious disaster that gives us unofficial authority to believe that we are paramount to everyone around us. There are things that you must be certain of but be careful of the manner in which you breathe this in. Be certain that humility and kindness will produce better results than maliciousness and selfishness. Be certain that the Divine assistance you appreciate comes not just in monetary gifts but various ways including smiles, laughter, words, and light. Be certain in your ability to express love to others more than just receiving it.

To be certain in a life of uncertainty requires awareness. There are at least 5 billion people in this world that believe in a God that is loving and just. Why then if you are created in this image, do you choose to act differently? Display how great the Creator is by the manner in which you express the gift of intellect given to you. You are certain of your God and the reflective image that you are, then show it! Know that in the midst of all calamity and chaos, there is a line that makes sense. You must find it. You must see the advantage in any eventuality.

There are always parallels moving together in this world. Bad and good, darkness and light are always in motion, unseen, but side by side. The defining moment is which one will be revealed by you. Which one will you allow to carry the balance and be manifested?

Certainty recognizes the consistent motion of how things change. It realizes the dichotomy of things intertwined and separate. Some things intermingled gives us joy:

Hot water + Cold water = warm water

Cocoa + Milk + Sugar = Milk Chocolate

Yellow + Blue = green

And other things are better left separate:

Oil + water

Bleach + Ammonia

But you are aware of these intertwined opposites that enliven our world.

TWENTY

CHAPTER 20   COURAGE AND DUTY
(Courage)

When people speak of courage, we instantly think about heroes (fictional or real) and believe that it is something that only lies in certain people. That is definitely not true. Courage is born of strength in mind and morality (to act on both), but it also implies that you are alert/aware. Heroes become so because they pay attention or notice things that others are unaware of. We must be aware of those things that can infect and affect us in any form. Those things that can pierce our beings or crush our bones must be recognized for their potential. It is about being aware of the fragility of being human.

Everyone possesses the ability to be courageous. Of course, police officers, firefighters, military personnel, nurses, doctors, are all seen as courageous but what about those that are hurt and rebound? People that lose limbs and decide not to allow it to impede their lives. Those that join the Special Olympics. When I see people that are hearing impaired, I do not see pity, I see people that have been given a deficiency yet they are more appreciative, vibrant, joyous than many of us with the ability to hear all of the noise around us.

You find out just how much courage that you truly have when you retain your standard when in combat. Not in a physical feud, but when you find yourself engaged in a verbal battle and powerful words are thrown at you, will you flee, fold, or stand? Courage requires you to be understanding in your thoughts. You must recognize that your position is not the only one that matters. People that have courage understand the fragility of not only the physical being but also the mental. This is why a truly courageous person is not a bully or a user of persons. Only people that fear you attempt to harm or misuse you.

What are you passionate about? Do you know or have you never considered what drives you? Being conscious of something that drives you, it allows you to be courageous in a moment of adversity.

COURAGE AND DUTY
(Duty)

What is your duty in this world and what are you bound to? You are bound to your Creator for giving you life. You are bound to your family for expressing love to you and giving you an outlet in which to act on your love. You are bound to yourself because your being is the apparatus in which thought is expressed into the physical realm. Although you may not believe that you have a duty, it is explained in everything around you. People say that the Creator is Life. Well, okay, how? The Divine created everything with parameters that protect it from premature expiration (death). You have natural filters in the body (liver, kidneys) that clean out the blood. When the body is harmed, it has a natural healing process that it goes through in order to continue its functions. The brain has indicators that alert the mind when pain or fear is imminent. The Creator has designed us with the intellect to recognize what is good for us and what is dangerous. You are duty-bound to live. That is your patented design.

Do not ever question or regret the assistance that you have given to another. You are obligated to aid those, even unawares, just as others have sacrificed for you. It is no longer just about you. It is about those that will come after you and depend upon you fulfilling your duty. Instinctively, humans seek to provide the safety and stability for their offspring. Just as all species attempt to allow their successors a chance at survival, humans too innately desire for our children to have the grounding to do and have what we could not. This is a natural duty built within all of us, recognized or not. We must stop failing in our general duties.

A duty is not an oppressive obligation. It is not necessary for you to feel angry or disgusted when you feel as though you should not be anchored to others because your duty is purposeful. I know that people are sick of clichés and the "everyone has a purpose" slogan is worn, but when you pay attention (exclude the noise in your mind) and see exactly how effectively you are in the lives of others, you become one with life. There is nothing living in this world that you are not connected to:

JOB 12:7-10

> "But now ask the beasts, and they will teach you; And the birds of the air, and they will tell you; Or speak to the earth, and it will teach you: And the fish of the sea will explain to you. Who among all these does not know that the hand of the Lord had done this, In whose hand is the life of every living thing, And the breath of all mankind?"

What one does will affect another, and what you refuse to do can destroy someone else's faith, hope, life. Choose to do something that will help another to live.

TWENTY ONE

BEING (TO BE) IS AN ACTIVE IDEA

THAT MAKES US ALIVE.

CHAPTER 21 IMPETUS TO ACT

The Love for Life must supersede the fear of death.

What is it that the human mind requires to move into action? Sometimes it can seem as though you have the drive of an Olympian and others you may feel as though why bother with anything? What makes you persevere when things are distraught and unclear? What unifies your thoughts into a cohesive funnel? Things that you are passionate about that have become interwoven into your design are those things that will encourage you. That thing that makes you emotional, that angers you when disturbed, that makes you joyous when blossomed, is what will push you and pull you into doing things never before achieved. When you are connected to your passion, there is an impulsive surge that goes through you that arouses your mind and spirit to do things not normally done.

Most of us fear dying. We are afraid to lose everything that we have and know. We don't want to lose this life because we are scared to death of what comes after. But people sacrifice their lives every day for various reasons. Some more noble than another but there is that one thing that will allow you to freely give up your life for it. Love, the chemical reaction, spiritual reaction, human attraction that is paramount to all fear. We all naturally have a protective guardian built inside that requires us to react (sometimes unaware) when we are needed.

John 15:13

"Greater Love hath no one than this, than to

lay down one's life for his friends."

The level of this relationship is extraordinary yet we see it all the time with our soldiers in combat, gangs in the streets or neighbors that support one another. But we must also realize that "laying down one's life" does not necessarily mean losing your life. Sacrificing for a friend is not always about dying. When you are so selfless with a friend that whatever they ask, you don't question it, you are laying down your life. You trust this person implicitly and you have no fear of betrayal or consequences. When you can totally sacrifice your all for another that is an exponential example of love.

Some people have never experienced this level of camaraderie. Why do you think that there are so many depressed and saddened people? As I've said, humans are interactive beings requiring social communication (or expressive) just as we do sunlight. When these beautiful children hurt themselves because of bullying, they always appear to feel alone. They always seem to think that there is no one that cares for them, even when they have a large family. Our impetus to act our love out in our daily affairs must not be impeded for fear of ridicule or harm. Or do you believe that there is no power in friendship? One of the greatest kings in history did;

2 Samuel 1:26

> "I am distressed for you, my brother
> Jonathan; You have been very pleasant to
> me; Your love to me was wonderful,
> surpassing the love of woman."

Paramount to most views is the concern for whom you call friend. Love of the opposite sex may cause you to do some crazy things but love of friendship can cause you to sacrifice everything.

TWENTY TWO

LOVE: THE CHEMICAL REACTION,

SPIRITUAL INTERACTION,

HUMAN ATTRACTION,

THAT OVERCOMES FEAR.

CHAPTER 22 WOMEN'S (R)EVOLUTION

When the idea of a revolution is spoken, we presume it is of a violent, aggressive, or antagonistic base. But as we think with a patient thought, we look at a revolution as not only a change in view but also a return to one's initial position. Our partnership with women is bonded with a shared spirit. The hateful view of women has been promulgated for centuries and is now being combated for its false origins. Women have been correlated with everything evil in this world and are continuously admonished that they are not as good as men. These wasteful ideas have lost their right and power to survive. The distortions of history and assumptions of what women can and cannot do are being revealed every day.

I believe that a unifying revolution is needed because we are in a time, an instance, when people are socially interactive whether they desire this or not. This is the inception of an era that will allow people to unite at every level of this planet. A revolution of this type mustn't be feared. It is not for revenge or the destruction of the masculine identity that this will happen, but for the insurance of human amelioration and elevation. Our survival has never been a singular race. It is not of a masculine dominance that we are excelling and progressing. It is only because of a shared and equal balance within our cultures that allow us to evolve. If women are inept, so too will the men be impotent.

A womans' position in life must not be demoted nor taken from her. She is an equal and interactive part of life. Her presence is required to fulfill humanity's duty. As I've displayed earlier, Eve's intent was neither deceptive nor malicious. Her intent was to improve her companion and her loyalty should be recognized more so than her naiveté. But the reality remains that it takes a colossal implosion to cause a shift. Women, like other minorities, have a myriad of factors that require their attention. They though, must not be afraid to combat these inconsistent prejudices at every stop. It is also important, and even pivotal, that those men who recognize those gender prejudices, must also attack them head on. This is about the improvement of life for all of us. Destruction, to women, to the poor, to the rich, to the blacks, to the Hispanics, and even to the politicians, is harmful to all of us.

In the Reciprocal Effect, I expressed how women, "give to us when they have nothing else to give and they love us even when we have not earned it". This is far from being a selfish person. This selfless spirit is seen in women (especially mothers) when they are involved with a project that they feel connected with. It is said that women are too emotional. Yes, well sometimes (or many times) men appear to be emotionless (until angered which has no limit of extremity). There must be a returning of the balance in a process that permits us growth. Women are the sense in the complexity that is our unit. They are the sense (rationality) in the complex (complicated whole). We must stop regarding them as an enemy and accept them as a partner.

The senseless destruction that targets women is suicide. This is not an extreme point of view but a realistic assessment of watching women struggle to maintain dignity, household, love, consciousness, and their womanhood. Woman, in maintaining her identity, has been impeded with every possible weapon yet she continues to persevere. She has continued to improve her status and the livelihood of our human race. The discriminatory cycle of women is not restricted by class or hue; it lives at all levels of life.

I recognize that men cannot excel with oppressed women. This is not feasible no matter how many believe the opposite. Kingdoms and nations are not great simply because the men were historic warriors or conquerors. First, all of these men had mothers that instilled principles within them. Others had lovers that envisioned their greatness and propelled them to excel. There is no man that has not been affected by a woman in some form. The vulnerability of men can only be properly shielded by that of a woman. That complimentary partner protects man from himself, his foes, and his anger. Why do you think that when man was created, the Creator said that it was not good for man to be alone? Isolation and loneliness create dismay and hollowness. This same isolation from the sensitivity of companionship permits the mind to justify callous behavior. If there is no balance within, then without will be totally anarchal. Men are not designed as impenetrable beings as women are not 'born simply to breed". That perfect relationship is how we are able to create evolving societies in our world. This is how we fully connect with the intellect that God has blessed us to tap into.

Both sides, masculine and feminine, are needed to keep everything working. Think of our everyday usage of things. Pipes must have both "male" and "female" components to connect in order for water, oil and other properties to flow over distances.

All things are evenly counter parted as this is the natural balance in which life is designed. We cannot function without the other in any way.

That is why I believe that a revolutionary call for women is needed now. An elevated roar for humanity to stand up and unite our commonality.

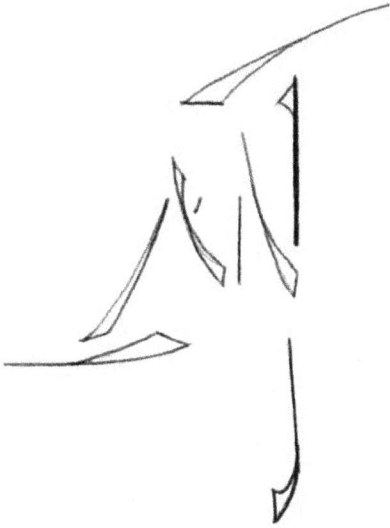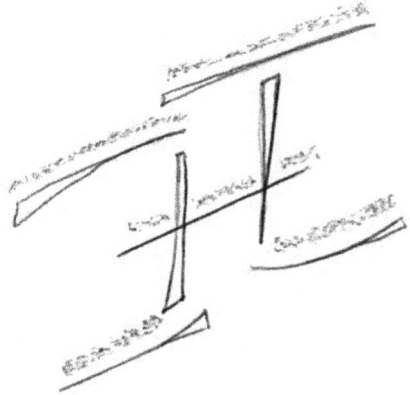

TWENTY THREE

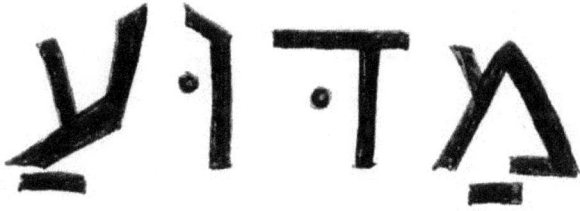

MADDUA

WHAT IS KNOWN?

CHAPTER 23   NOW WHAT?

So, what are you going to do now? No, what are you doing right now? Sitting around complaining about why the world is against you or laying by as time continues to lose you in its eternal existence. There is no more room for unconscious efforts. No more margin for senseless (inept) actions that produce nothing. If we are to continue to evolve forward and pass this decadent state, then we must not allow our past (or present) to continue blurring our future. We must set standards for ourselves that we will adhere to. Make them so that we don't find excuses around them. We must tell ourselves right now, no more. Whatever it is that has us bound, whatever has a grip upon us, whatever has us netted, we must stop allowing it to do so. Only those that are slaves to something are not permitted to separate from that which is harboring them.

Who do you want to be: The image or the person? How do you want your family to view you? How do you want to view yourself? Stop telling yourself what you are not and begin appreciating what you are. Invoke that sleeping spirit within you and believe in its connection to everything around you. You must make the decision and apply it in real time. All of your credit (excuses) is in debt.

You must acquire the confidence and control (of your mind) to make your applied ideas a reality.

PROVERBS 19:15

> "Laziness casts one into a deep sleep, and an
> idle person will suffer hunger."

You are living in a time when information is easily ascertained. A time when entrepreneurship is not foreign or restricted to some unseen hierarchy with unlimited wealth and knowledge. It is no longer about the place of your birth or the manner of your faith. It is about who you are and how you will apply what you know. You are only restricted by your ability to be deterred in manifesting your tasks. I inquire again, who do you want to be, the person or the image?

Now is the time for you to say that, "I am sick of doing nothing!" Now is the time to recognize that you are a complete being that has the creative potential (ability) to outmaneuver any problem. The source of your energy, the link to your creative authority, the anchor to your spiritual sanity is always present in you. It is up to you to pay attention to it.

You are living right now. Your existence is alive right at this time. The selective decisions that you choose will either aid your joy or cripple it. Your awareness will allow you to conquer the tragedies that attack you. Avoid unnecessary things, don't acknowledge distractions that are deteriorating. This world, in all of its brightness, color, and technology is filled with things that keep your mind so occupied that it enslaves itself.

I know. Sometimes you feel as though you are not smart enough, strong enough, disciplined, or courageous enough to implement your ideas. Well, that is just another distraction that is easier to succumb to than the others. No more of these weak problems that you allow to defeat you before you even begin. No more of these ideas that you are not capable of being that great being. Now is the time to begin. Now is that moment when you can complement that goal in which you have set. Remember, you are the jailer, the regulator, the liberator, the one who chooses to be the human design, or the copy?

The following 15 ideas are things that I believe that we must continuously invoke in one another in order to stay progressive and inspired. Being involved with others on even the most ordinary level, a smile, a conversation, or a relationship, involves sharing thoughts and energy. People do not understand one another because we don't talk to one another. The ideology of human assumption preceeds all of our lifetimes but we don't have to give it life. Right now, ask yourself do you believe in the power and intelligence of the One that created all things around you? If you do, then now, right now is the moment in which you must be who you were designed to be.

N. Malaki Crayton

INSPIRING GENERATIONS

1. Destroy the perception of stereotypes. Stop acting out these flaws simply because we are labeled them. When they are continuously admonished that they are bad, they will act out as such.

2. No more tolerance for negative ideas that are accepted by the people. We must eradicate bad ideas with better ideas and stop accepting things that we know to be wrong.

3. Our ideas and actions must be correlated and funneled together so that we can actively produce effective results.

4. We must stop unnecessary complaining which is only comparable with another complaint. This births an insatiable appetite that allows failure to be that much easier.

5. Those in positive positions must stay innovative, influential and focused because their fall would cause an immeasurable damaging effect within these communities.

6. Young adults are easily distracted and we must hold their attention with things that grasp their interests because once they are bored, they are easily swayed.

7. We must learn to ask for and accept assistance, not necessarily charity. This recognizes that we perform these tasks, not out of pity, but out of our responsibility to each other.

8. We have to stop being so rash to speak on inflammatory rumors and slander for sport. These turn into deadly results

as people may not be able to decipher fact from fiction.

9. If you don't have the patience to look at the problem, you will never uncover the solution within it.

10. To keep our work from warping later on, our foundation must be able to evolve and absorb the shocks of an ever changing world.

11. They must be shown the value of their lives and what they mean to this world. Help them understand the world that they live in.

12. We must be successful. If we have nothing to offer them (Spiritually, financially, emotionally), they will not be attentive.

13. We must be articulate and persuasive but not foreign in our language. Struggling for their minds will take influence.

14. They must see civil adults as a real power, a credible hierarchy worthy of their respect.

15. We must be precise and to the point. If our direction (or actions) is drawn out and unclear, they will grow tired of aimless wandering.

ABOUT THE AUTHOR

This book is not about me but showing that human compassion and camaraderie exceeds all limits. We must recognize as a human family that bad ideas that harm us must not be allowed to succeed. This book was compiled to show you, the reader, that even in the harshest of places, positive ideas are still effective. Apply it and manifest yours.